Dudley Baxter

National income

The United Kingdom

Dudley Baxter

National income
The United Kingdom

ISBN/EAN: 9783337137588

Printed in Europe, USA, Canada, Australia, Japan

Cover: Foto ©Suzi / pixelio.de

More available books at **www.hansebooks.com**

NATIONAL INCOME.

THE UNITED KINGDOM.

BY

R. DUDLEY BAXTER, M.A.

READ BEFORE THE STATISTICAL SOCIETY OF LONDON,

JANUARY 21, 1868.

London :

MACMILLAN AND CO.

1868.

LONDON:

R. CLAY, SON, AND TAYLOR, PRINTERS,

BREAD STREET HILL.

INTRODUCTION.

THERE is in the Atlantic an island—the Peak of Teneriffe—which rises from the sea in a pyramidal form to the height of 12,000 feet, conspicuous from every point of the horizon, and casting its shadow from the morning or evening sun for fifty miles over the ocean. An inhabitant is scarcely aware of its real proportions : for if he lives at its foot, he sees chiefly the lower eminences which rise immediately above him ; and if he climbs the heights he is apt to lose sight of the broad base which spreads below. He must leave the land and sail out into the offing, before he can form any accurate picture of the real outline, and grasp as a whole the shape and majesty of his mountain isle. I have often thought that such an island is a good emblem of a wealthy state, with its long low base of labouring population, with its uplands of the middle classes, and with the towering peaks and summits of those with princely incomes. The difficulty is, to ascertain the

B

relative dimensions of these mountain zones. If
we take our stand on the lower plateau we are
absorbed in its extent and richness, and cannot see
or appreciate the ridges which rise tier upon tier
above us; and if we devote ourselves to exploring
and measuring the higher ranges we are prone to
overlook and despise the plains far below us. We
must sail out into the offing, till we can see the
island as one grand whole, and realize its true
proportions.

Questions proposed.   There can scarcely be an inquiry more interesting to those who take a pride in their country
than the investigation of the statistics of our
National Income. What are the means and aggregate wages of our labouring population; what the
numbers and aggregate profits of the middle classes;
what the revenues of our great proprietors and
capitalists; and what the pecuniary strength of the
nation to bear the burdens annually falling upon
us? What capital in land and goods and money is
stored up for our subsistence, and for carrying out
our enterprises? What is the relative magnitude of
our National Debt? What progress has been made
since the beginning of the century in the increase
of our income and the accumulation of savings?
And what are the risks to which our wealth is
exposed, and the precautions that ought to be

taken for our own protection and for the safety of posterity ?

The materials for such an inquiry are abundantly Data available. ample ; but their enormous mass renders it difficult to present them clearly and in small compass. The long catalogue of occupations of the people, and the infinite variety of wages even in the same occupations, can only be appreciated by those who have endeavoured to reduce them to order. Minute accuracy is unattainable, and we are obliged to work by general averages. The great object is to render those averages trustworthy and simple, and that they should not be undigested masses of figures, of mere lists of unconnected totals, but coherent and lucid. Nor ought important facts to rest upon mere assertion ; the authorities for the facts, and the reasons for the calculations, ought in every case to be given, so that the reader may refer and verify for himself.

Such an inquiry involves important questions of Political Economy. Political Economy. But Political Economy ought to mingle in all such discussions. Statistics are a storehouse of examples in Economical Science. Statistics are the mathematical expression of classes of economical facts. They contain those facts in the briefest possible summary, like a landscape condensed into a miniature photograph. But, like

miniature photographs, they require a microscope to
bring out their full significance.   Any inquiry that
does this must afford valuable matter for Political
Economists—facts by which to test the truth of
their theories, and the means by which they may
extend their discoveries.   Such is the ideal at
which a statistical paper should aim, although I
dare not hope that I have attained it in the present
effort.

PART I.

Classification of the Population.

CHAPTER I.

THE INCOME-CLASSES.

THE first step towards a reliable estimate of the CHAP. I.
Income of a nation is to ascertain the number
of individuals who possess or earn it. This can be
done for the United Kingdom from the Census Division
Tables of 1861, which give in very great detail the tion into
occupations of the people, and the number of Classes
persons engaged in each. From them it is possible pendent
to ascertain, with tolerable accuracy, the number of Classes.
persons who may be presumed to have independent
incomes or wages. They are as follows :—

POPULATION OF ENGLAND AND WALES, 1861.   Appendix
I.

I. *Persons with Incomes or Wages* (Men, boys,
women, and girls)   9,289,000
II. *Persons without Incomes or Wages*   .   . 10,626,000

Total accounted for -   . 19,915,000

`Besides 151,000 respecting whom nothing was ascertained.

If we could obtain the average income of each
occupation we should be able to deduce the aggre-

gate income of the nation. This method is practicable for the occupation pursued by the Manual Labour Class, whose wages are generally at average rates, known to their employers. But it fails with those above the Manual Labour Class, whose earnings are much more variable, and whose incomes are in great part derived from capital. It becomes necessary, therefore, to make a further classification of the persons with independent incomes into the *Upper and Middle Classes* on the one hand, and the *Manual Labour Class* on the other. I purposely adopt the latter term, as less ambiguous than *Working Classes.* This classification has been worked out for each of the three kingdoms, and summaries of its method and results are given for England and Wales in Appendix I. Their great bulk renders it impossible to print a larger portion.

As regards England and Wales the result is as follows. Putting together all ages and sexes, the totals are :—

Upper and Middle Classes and Manual Labour Class.

England and Wales.

Appendix I. Table 1.

PERSONS WITH INCOMES OR WAGES.

ENGLAND AND WALES, 1861.

	Persons.
1. *Upper and Middle Classes*	1,943,000
2. *Manual Labour Class*	7,346,000
Total . .	9,289,000

So that the Upper and Middle Classes with Chap. I. incomes of their own, are rather more than one-fifth of the total Income-Classes, or one-fourth of the similar members of the Manual Labour Class.

These were the numbers in 1861. But since that Increase since 1861. time six years have elapsed, and there is an increase to be allowed for. During the decade from 1851 to 1861 the increase of the population in England and Wales was 12 per cent., being rather less than that in previous decades. To be safe we will take the increase of the Income-Classes during the last six years at only 6 per cent. That increase will amount to 550,000, and by the proportions just established must be divided as follows :—

INCREASE OF INCOME-CLASSES.

ENGLAND AND WALES, 1861 TO 1867.

	Persons.
Upper and Middle Classes (one-fifth) . . .	110,000
Manual Labour Class (four-fifths) . . .	440,000
Total Increase . .	550,000

Thus, since 1861, more than 500,000 additional persons have been thrown into the labour-field, to compete with the former number of professional men, tradesmen, clerks, and manual labourers in England and Wales ; and these 500,000 must find themselves employment under penalty of starvation. In a whole decade, as from 1861 to 1871, more

CHAP. I. than *a million* of additional workers are thrown
into competition with the number existing at
the beginning of the period. They are not new
workers to supply death-vacancies, but new workers
in addition to those who fill up death-vacancies.
The struggle for life of plants and animals, pointed
out by Mr. Darwin, could scarcely be more severe.
This enormous and constant importation into the
labour-market must always be borne in mind in
considering the question of deficient work and
average earnings.

Income
Classes.
Scotland
and
Ireland.
As regards Scotland and Ireland, the classification has been made on the same method, allowing
in the case of Ireland for the larger number of
small farmers, who are about 73 per cent. of the
whole class. The results will be found in Tables
1 and 2 of Appendix I., but their purport may
be briefly stated as showing that in all the three
kingdoms the Income-Classes, or persons with
independent incomes or wages, bear nearly the
same proportion to the whole population. The

United
Kingdom.
total for the United Kingdom is :—

POPULATION OF UNITED KINGDOM, 1861.

1. Persons with Incomes or Wages . .	13,270,000
2. Persons without Incomes or Wages . .	15,507,000
Total accounted for . .	28,777,000

Being 46 per cent. and 54 per cent. of the total ; CHAP. I.
or a little more than five persons with income or
wages to every six persons without income through-
out the whole kingdom.

As regards the division of Income-Classes into Upper and
the Upper and Middle Classes and Manual Labour and
Class, in Scotland the Upper and Middle Classes Labour
had in 1861, 264,000 persons with incomes of their Scotland.
own against 1,089,000 earners of the Manual
Labour Class.

And in Ireland they had 452,000 persons with Ireland.
incomes against 2,175,000 earners of the Manual
Labour Class.

For the United Kingdom the numbers were :— United
Kingdom.

PERSONS WITH INCOMES OR WAGES.

UNITED KINGDOM, 1861.

	Persons.
1. Upper and Middle Classes	2,660,000
2. Manual Labour Class	10,610,000
Total .	13,270,000

Being 20 per cent. against 80 per cent., or one-
fifth and four-fifths, as in England.

In Scotland the rate of increase of the popu- Increase of
lation is only half that of England, or 6 per cent. population.
in the ten years. Emigration has something to Scotland.
do with this, for the Scotchman retains the cha-

CHAP. I. racteristic observed by Dr. Johnson, of fondness for the road to England ; and has added a fondness for the road to India. Besides this, the Scot is a cautious man, and is made doubly cautious by the looseness of the marriage laws. The increase of the Scotch Income-Classes, from 1861 to 1867, need only be estimated at 3 per cent., or 40,000.

Decrease. Ireland.

In Ireland there has been a decrease of 4 per cent., or 241,000, as estimated by the Registrar General.

Income Classes.

In all these estimates of the persons with independent income or earnings I have included every person, of whatever age or sex, who is returned in the Census Tables as following any distinct occupation ; and have added part of the widows, who

See Appendix I. Table 4.

must of necessity have some kind of income, and in a few instances part of the wives.

CHAPTER II.

THE UPPER AND MIDDLE CLASSES AND THE MANUAL LABOUR CLASS.

BEFORE plunging into the question of Incomes, I CHAP. II.
should like to digress for a short time to a point of
great interest, viz. to endeavour to determine the
total numbers, including families, of the Upper and Total
Middle Classes and the Manual Labour Class of Upper and
Middle
England and Wales. The calculation has often Classes and
Manual
been made on conjectural grounds, and with the Labour
Class,
most diverse results, usually varying according to England
and
the personal predilections of the calculator. The Wales.
first Table given in the Appendix affords the
means of ascertaining their numbers with something like certainty. It gives the total number
of males above twenty years of age who in the
Census Tables of 1861 have occupations belonging Appendix
I.
to the Upper and Middle Classes; and shows Table 1.
their number to be 1,194,000. But the males

CHAP. II. above twenty years of age bear a known proportion to the total population, being as nearly as possible twenty-six per cent., or in round numbers one-fourth. So that we may with accuracy calculate the total numbers of the Upper and Middle Classes at a little less than four times the number of their adult males. Then by subtraction from the total population we can find the total number of the Manual Labour Classes. Performing these operations, and adding six per cent. for the increase since 1861, we find that in England and Wales, out of a total population in 1867 of 21,000,000, the Upper and Middle Classes were 4,870,000 and the Manual Labour Class 16,130,000.

Houses of Upper and Middle Classes, 1,110,000.
It is a confirmation of these figures that the number of £10 houses in boroughs and counties of England and Wales in the Electoral Returns of 1866 (allowing 50,000 for the difference between rating and rental in the counties) was 1,250,000, of which about 140,000 were occupied by the Manual Labour Class. The remainder, or 1,110,000 houses, correspond nearly with the 4,870,000 persons of the Upper and Middle Classes, and with their servants.

The complete table is as follows :—

ENGLAND AND WALES, 1867. CHAP. II.

UPPER AND MIDDLE AND MANUAL LABOUR CLASSES.

Upper and Middle Classes—   Persons.
With Independent Incomes . . 2,053,000
Dependent 2,817,000
——— 4,870,000
Manual Labour Class—
Earning Wages 7,785,000
Dependent 8,345,000
——— 16,130,000
Total Population of England
and Wales, 1867 . 21,000,000

Hence the Upper and Middle Classes are 5,000,000
in round numbers, and have nearly three persons
dependent for every two with independent income.

The Manual Labour are 16,000,000 in round
numbers, and are almost equally divided between
earners and non-earners.

In Scotland the same data and principles of Scotland.
calculation, with 3 per cent. increase of population, give—

SCOTLAND, 1867.
                                            Persons.
Upper and Middle Classes 692,000
Manual Labour Class 2,460,000
Total Population, 1867 . . 3,152,000

CHAP. II.   The proportions between the independent incomes or earners and the dependent persons in each class, are the same as in England.

Ireland.   In Ireland the same calculation, but with 4 per cent. decrease of population, gives—

IRELAND, 1867.

					Persons.
Upper and Middle Classes	.	.	.	.	1,056,000
Manual Labour Class	.	.	.	.	4,501,000
Total Population, 1867 .			. .		5,557,000

United Kingdom.   For the United Kingdom the several Classes are as follows :—

UNITED KINGDOM, 1867.

		Persons.
Upper and Middle Classes—		
With Independent Incomes	. 2,759,000	
Dependent	. 3,859,000	
		6,618,000
Manual Labour Class—		
Earning Wages . . .	. 10,961,000	
Dependent	. 12,130,000	
		23,091,000
Total Estimated Population .		29,709,000

The per centages are—Upper and Middle Classes, 23 per cent. ; Manual Labour Class, 77 per cent.

Putting the result into round numbers, out of a total population of 30,000,000, the Upper and Middle Classes are 7,000,000 and the Manual Labour Class 23,000,000.

Recurring to the simile in which I compared the State to an island ; rather more than three-fourths of its surface is formed by the Manual. Labour Class, and rather less than one-fourth by the Upper and Middle Classes.

PART II.

Income of the United Kingdom.

c 2

CHAPTER III.

UPPER AND MIDDLE INCOMES.

WE have now to ascertain the incomes of the Upper and Middle Classes. This can only be done through the Income Tax—an impost which is their peculiar burden, and one in which very few workmen, however high their wages, ever allow themselves to be caught. An Assessor told me that he had often in his district working men who he knew must be in receipt of more than £100, but whom he never could succeed in assessing. As every one is aware, the Income Tax commences at £100 a year, but allows a deduction of £60 from all incomes below £200. For convenience of reference I give the five Schedules into which it is divided :

Schedule A.   .   Lands (owners), Houses, Railways, Mines, &c.

    „   B.   .   Lands (occupiers ; on half the rent).

    „   C.   .   Public Funds (British, Foreign and Colonial).

    „   D.   .   Trades and Professions, and Foreign Property.

    „   E.   .   Public Offices (General, Local, and Railway).

NOTE.—An Act of 1866 transferred railways, mines, ironworks, and miscellaneous property to Schedule D, leaving only land and houses in Schedule A. For uniformity I adhere to the old classification.

Margin notes: CHAP. III. Income Tax peculiar to the Upper and Middle Classes. Distinction between gross and net numbers.

CHAP. III.   A man may be assessed under two or more of these Schedules, so that the total of the numbers of ultimate tax-payers in each Schedule by no means represents the net number of individuals charged. A memorandum will be found in the Appendix, the substance of which was communicated to me by Mr. Gripper of the Inland Revenue, the highest authority in all statistics of that department, in which the net number of Income tax-payers is computed, and their average income in England and Wales calculated at £306, after making allowance for the number of additional persons who pay in companies or partnerships.

The latest return of Income charged to Income Tax is for the financial year 1865.

INCOME TAX.—UNITED KINGDOM.

Property and Income *charged to Duty* under each Schedule of the Income-Tax Act for the Year 1865, ended 5th April 1866:—

Schedule	Amount of Property and Income charged in			
	England.	Scotland.	Ireland.	United Kingdom.
A . .	125,143,490	15,099,198	13,876,913	154,119,601
B . .	28,890,437	3,717,195	2,956,643	35,564,275
C . .	31,930,560	—	1,140,120	33,070,680
D . .	103,908,302	10,942,857	5,296,536	120,147,695
E . .	19,302,458	1,057,308	1,168,536	21,528,302
Total .	£309,175,247	30,816,558	24,438,748	364,430,553

Thus the Income of the United Kingdom in Chap. III.
1865, which actually paid Income Tax, was Additions
£364,430,000. What additions must be made to ^{up to 1867.}
arrive at the total Income in 1867 of the Upper and
Middle Classes? The inquiry involves many interesting points in the history of our financial progress.

Ever since the imposition of the Income Tax in Constant
1842, there has been a continual increase in the _{increase of} Income
charged.
amount of property assessed. For the first ten
years, 1842 to 1852, the augmentation in England and Wales was very slow, being less than
£6,000,000, or an average of £600,000 a year.
In Scotland it was more rapid, being more than
£4,000,000, or an average of £400,000 a year on
one-tenth of the amount of income. The total Seventh
Inland
increase for Great Britain during those ten years Revenue
Report,
was about £10,285,000, or £1,000,000 a year. p. 23.

In 1853 the Income Tax was extended to Ireland,
and was brought down from incomes of £150 to
£100. The rapid progress of commerce, conse-
quent upon the development of the railway system
at home and abroad, and free trade legislation,
produced a corresponding increase in the property
charged; and down to 1865 this increase has gone
on in a continually augmenting ratio. In 1855 Tenth
Inland
the property charged to duty in the United King- Revenue
Report.
dom, under the new law, was £268,300,000; in

1865 it had risen to £364,430,000 ; being a total increase in ten years of £96,000,000, or an average increase of nearly £10,000,000 a-year.

Land, &c.: Schedule A.

But to understand the nature of this increase, we must examine the schedules of the Income Tax. *Land and houses, railways and mines, and other real property,* have been included, down to 1866, in Schedule A, and have been remarkable for the steadiness with which they have increased in value. A revaluation has been made every fourth year, and latterly every third year, and the last three revaluations, in 1857, 1861, and 1864, each added nearly £12,000,000 to the total property charged to duty, being at the rate of £3,000,000 a year at the commencement of thë period, in 1853, and at the rate of £4,000,000 a year at its close. This increase represents a *profitable* investment in houses, railways, mines, and agricultural and other improvements of *Capital,* to an average amount of £80,000,000 in each year.

Out of the £12,000,000 increase of income, shown by revaluation every third or fourth year under this schedule, land produces £2,000,000, or one-sixth, augmenting its total value at the rate of one per cent. per annum ; houses produce £6,500,000, or one-half, augmenting their total value at the rate of 3½ per cent. per annum ; and railways, mines, quarries, and similar property, yield the remaining CHAP. III. £3,500,000, or one-third, raising their total value at the rate of 6½ per cent. per annum. Thus, five-sixths of the capital annually invested in permanent improvements is laid out in houses and railways, and similar works.

The year 1867 happens to have been the revaluation year, and may be expected to produce an increase of at least £12,000,000 over the total property charged under Schedule A in 1864.

Farmers' profits, measured by ~~half~~ their rentals under Schedule B, have increased from £30,200,000 charged to duty in 1855 to £35,550,000 in 1865. The increase has taken place almost entirely in revaluation years, and is very small, or a decrease, in the intervening years. The increase in valuations was—

Farmers' profits: Schedule B.

INCREASE OF INCOME CHARGED IN SCHEDULE B.

		£
1857 over 1853	. . . . . .	3,000,000
1861	. . . .	2,300,000
1864	. . . .	700,000

—a declining ratio which looks as if farmers' rents are near their maximum, and which I commend to the notice of Chambers of Agriculture. It would seem that we cannot count on an increase of more than £700,000 in the revaluation year 1867.

Income derived from *Funds (British, Colonial,*

CHAP. III.
Funds:
Schedule
C.

and Foreign) is charged under Schedule C, and has increased from £25,778,000 in 1855 to £33,070,000 in 1865, or an average increase of £700,000 a year. The increase since 1861 has been very regular in amount. It indicates Foreign and Colonial Loans of about £15,000,000 yearly.

Public
Offices :
Schedule
E.

Income from *Salaries and Pensions* is charged under Schedule E, and increased from £17,000,000 in 1855, to £20,700,000 in 1862, then diminishing for two years, and again rising, in 1865, to £21,528,000. An increase during the last two years may be expected from increased local government and railway offices, but is uncertain in amount.

Trades and
Profes-
sions :
Schedule
D.

But Income from *Trades and Professions,* charged under Schedule D, is the gauge of the prosperity of the nation. It is the least reliable of all the schedules, because depending so much upon the will of the person assessed. It is the most variable in amount, because of the fluctuations in profit in different years. But excessive fluctuation is avoided by the provision entitling persons to be charged on the average of the three preceding years, with an option to claim an abate-

Dr. Farr,
Income
Committee
Report,
1861, p.
171.

ment if the profit of the year of payment is below the average. The result is to give the tax-payer the advantage of his minimum income, and to deprive the country of the advantage of his maximum CHAP. III. income. The amount of Income charged under Schedule D varies with almost every cause affecting . the wealth of the nation, but principally with the foreign trade. The rate of discount has not a very visible effect upon it. The Income charged to duty in the United Kingdom rose from £79,000,000 in 1855, to £120,000,000 in 1865 ; being a total increase of £41,000,000 in ten years, or an average of £4,000,000 a year. The following table shows its fluctuations, and those of the Exports and Imports.

INCREASE OF INCOME CHARGED IN SCHEDULE D AND OF EXPORTS, AND IMPORTS.—UNITED KINGDOM.

Year.	Increase or Decrease of Imports and Exports.	Increase of Income charged to Schedule D.	
	£	£	
1855	— 8,000,000 (decrease)	—	Crimean War.
1856	+51,000,000 (increase)	1,360,000	
1857	+22,000,000	4,480,000	
1858	—29,600,000 (decrease)	90,000	Panic.
1859	+30,500,000 (increase)	4,190,000	
1860	+40,200,000	600,000	{ French Treaty. { Chinese War.
1861	+ 2,000,000	4,089,000	
1862	+14,800,000	4,300,000	
1863	+53,900,000	2,220,000	Cotton Famine.
1864	+41,700,000	9,890,000	
1865	+ 2,300,000	10,040,000	Ditto and Panic.
1866	+44,100,000		
1867	— (decrease)		

CHAP. III.   This table shows the augmented ratio of progress in the latter years. The first five years included two wars and a panic, and produced a total increase of nearly £11,000,000, or £2,000,000 a year. The second five years included three years of cotton famine and one of panic, and produced a total increase of £30,000,000, or £6,000,000 a year.

Estimated increase for 1866 and 1867.   It is impossible to form any judgment from the Revenue returns of the increase or decrease during 1866 and 1867, since the quarterly statements for 1866 contain a portion of the sixpenny tax of 1865, and the collection of Income Tax for the last quarter of 1867 was deferred to 1868 in consequence of the revaluation. This is the explanation of the apparent diminution in the returns published for the Christmas quarter. There is no doubt that the rate of increase will be considerably diminished. But from other data, the healthy state of the foreign trade, and the large Exports and Imports, we shall be justified in estimating a total increase for the two years of £4,000,000, being only one-fifth of that for the two preceding years. .

The total increase estimated for 1866 and 1867 on all the schedules is shown in Table 1 of Appendix V., and amounts to £14,000,000, which

should be divided between the three Kingdoms, in CHAP. III.
the proportions of England and Wales £12,200,000 ;
Scotland £1,500,000 ; Ireland £300,000.

But before leaving this part of the subject Ten years'
it may be useful to glance at the following table, 1855—
drawn up from the Tenth Inland Revenue Report, 1865.
showing the distribution in the Schedules of the
increase of £96,000,000 from 1855 to 1865.

TEN YEARS' INCREASE OF INCOME CHARGED TO INCOME TAX,
1855—1865.

UNITED KINGDOM.

Schedule A—	£	£
Land	6,400,000	
Houses	19,000,000	
Railways, Mines, &c. . .	12,250,000	
		37,650,000
Schedule B—Farmers		5,350,000
„ C—Foreign and Colonial Funds . .		7,300,000
„ D—Trades and Professions and Foreign Property		41,200,000
„ E—Public Offices		4,500,000
		£96,000,000

This increase was produced by the three kingdoms
in the following proportions :—

	£
England and Wales	84,000,000
Scotland	8,700,000
Ireland	3,300,000
	£96,000,000

The important nature of this increase can scarcely be exaggerated. During the ten years from 1842 to 1852 the income of Great Britain charged to Income Tax increased £10,000,000, being nearly 4 per cent. or *one-twenty-fifth.* During the ten years from 1855 to 1865 the Income of the United Kingdom charged to Income Tax increased £96,000,000, being 36 per cent. on the £268,000,000 which paid duty in 1855, or more than *one-third.*

The average income of each person in the United Kingdom who paid duty under Schedule D in 1855, was £288. In 1864, the latest year for which the numbers are given, it had risen to £314.

Using these figures as a means of measuring the whole Income Tax in 1855 and 1865, the proportion (not the actual number) of Income tax-payers will have risen from 931,000 in 1855 to 1,160,000 in 1865. This was an increase of 229,000, or 25 per cent., the increase of the population during the same period for Great Britain (exclusive of Ireland) being 11 per cent.

The addition during these ten years to the profitable Capital of the Upper and Middle Class Income tax-payers, by increased value of their real property and by foreign loans and property and accumulation of floating capital, indicated in the

above figures for Schedules A, B, C, and D only,
is about *twelve hundred millions sterling*, or 120
millions a year. Table 2.

All these amounts are irrespective of any increase in the income, or earnings, or the property of the rest of the population who do not pay Income Tax, and were confined simply to the Income Tax payers. Nor even as regards them do these numbers represent the real increase. They are merely the amounts shown by the unwilling returns of those tax-payers, and on which they cannot escape the assessments of the Government.

It is as if the island of the State had been subject to an upheaval, slow at first, but increasing in rapidity, which has brought a circle of fresh lands above the surface of the waves, and raised to more commanding heights its hills and mountain summit. How long this upheaval and increase will last, and at what rate, is beyond human power to predict. England is more favourably situated than any country, except the United States, for manufactures and commerce ; and the demand for these must augment continually with the spread of civilization and railways among the 1,200,000,000 population of the world. The future rise of the United States into a great manufacturing and naval power, appears the most probable and certain cause

CHAP. III. which will place a limit to our national increase and prosperity.

Unreturned profits.

We now come to a second class of additions, and must take into account the *Unreturned Profits* of trades and professions, and other incomes under Schedule D. Mr. Lowe's Draft Report to the Income Tax Committee of 1861 thus describes it: —" Schedule D depends on the conscience of the tax-payer, who often, it is to be feared, returns hundreds instead of thousands, and who is certain to decide any question that he can persuade himself to think doubtful, in his own favour." The extent to which he may exonerate himself can be judged from the following facts.

First Inland Revenue Report.

In 1799, all Income Tax-payers assessed themselves. In 1803, the present schedules were introduced, and the system was changed, except for Schedule D, to payment of duty by the occupier or first source. The effect was to make the produce of the tax at 5 per cent. in 1803, almost equal to that at 10 per cent. in 1799. In other words, the alteration increased the amount collected by 100 per cent.

An improved method and greater experience in collection prevents the evil from attaining such proportions in the present day, but Mr.

Budget Speeches.

Gladstone in his Budget Speech for 1853 gave a remarkable instance of the prevalence of the

practice. Twenty-eight persons claimed com- CHAP. III.
pensation for loss of business by the construc-
tion of Cannon Street in the City. They claimed
£48,159 as one year's profits ; and obtained from
the jury £26,973, or a little more than half.
They had returned their profits to the Income
Tax at £9,000! I am told on the highest authority that in a single day two cheques were
sent in to the Chancellor of the Exchequer for
£9,000 and £2,300 for unreturned Income Tax.

It is a very moderate estimate to place the unreturned profits at 16 per cent. on the £100,000,000
charged in England and Wales under Schedule D,
and at 10 per cent. for Scotland and Ireland.

Another addition must be made for the £60 £60 a-year
a year excused to incomes between £100 and Inland excused.
£200. It amounted in 1864 to £12,375,000. Revenue, Tenth
Report, p.
A third class of additions still remains. A very 42.
large number of the Middle Classes have incomes Incomes
of less than £100 a year, and are not included £100. less than
in the Income Tax returns. Their numbers can
be found for each of the three kingdoms by subtraction of the Income tax-payers from the total
number of the Upper and Middle Classes who
have independent incomes.

There is little doubt that large numbers of them
are at or near £100, either on one side or the

CHAP. III. other of the line, and the salaries and board of few of them will in England be less than £50. It appears a safe calculation to place their average actual earnings or income in England and Wales, after a considerable deduction for want of employment, at £60 a year.

England and Wales.   Hence for England and Wales the Upper and Middle Incomes will be as follows :—

Gross Income.

GROSS INCOME OF THE UPPER AND MIDDLE CLASSES, 1867.

ENGLAND AND WALES.

	£
I.—*Incomes charged to Income Tax*—	
1. Income Tax was charged in 1865 on	309,000,000
2. The increase 1865 to 1867 may be taken at	12,200,000
So that the total amount charged in 1867 would be	321,200,000

This amount at an average of £306 would be paid by 1,050,000 persons.

But there are 2,053,000 persons of the Upper and Middle Classes with independent Incomes, allowing 110,000 for the increase since 1861; so that 1,003,000 are not included in the Income Tax.

	£
3. Unreturned profits under Schedule D	16,000,000
4. The £60 a year excused to Incomes between £100 and £200	10,000,000
II.—*Incomes not charged to Income Tax*—	
5. The 1,003,000 persons under £100 a year at £60 each	60,000,000
Total	£407,200,000

But in order to gain a clear idea of this wealth, Chap. III. we must ascertain the manner in which it is distributed among the different classes of income, as Distribution of £100 to £300 a-year; £300 to £1,000; £1,000 to Income. £5,000; and £5,000 and upwards. This can be done for Schedule D, from the official returns :—

DISTRIBUTION OF INCOME—SCHEDULE D.

CLASS OF INCOME.	PER CENTAGES.	
	Assessments.	Aggregate Income.
£5,000 to £50,000 and upwards . .	·7	32
£1,000 to £5,000	4·	20
£300 to £1,000	14·3	21
£100 to £300	81·	27

We may fairly assume that a similar proportion obtains in the aggregate of all the schedules of the Income Tax. Working this out, and adding the Incomes below the Income Tax, *i.e.* under £100 a year, we have the following table :—

CHAP. III.   UPPER AND MIDDLE CLASSES: DISTRIBUTION OF INCOMES.
ENGLAND AND WALES, 1867.

CLASS OF INCOME.	Number of Assessments.	Aggregate Annual Income.
I. *Large Incomes—*		£
(1) £5,000 to £50,000 and upwards	7,500	111,104,000
(2) £1,000 to £5,000 . .	42,000	69,440,000
II. *Middle Incomes—*		
£300 to £1,000 . , . .	150,000	72,912,000
III. *Small Incomes—*		
(1) £100 to £300	850,500	93,744,000
(2) Below the Income Tax, under £100	1,003,000	60,000,000
Total . . . . ,	2,053,000	£407,200,000

This classification is subject to a disturbing element, the presence in the incomes above £5,000 of 350 Companies with £28,000,000 income, each paying Income Tax at their head office, as one person. Few people have all their property invested in these Companies, but a very large number of incomes are lessened in the returns by a portion of their amount being assessed through a Company. If the Companies' incomes were distributed to the individuals to which they belong, a considerable number of persons would be raised out of each class into the next above ; so that, for example, the £5,000 class would be enlarged in numbers more than sufficient to compensate for the loss of the assessments of Companies. Partnerships, on the contrary, raise incomes into higher classes than the individual partners would reach. I have pointed out in Appendix II. that the diminution of numbers by assessments on partnerships is compensated by individuals being very commonly assessed under two or even three Schedules for different portions of their income.

The general correctness of the numbers in the above table is confirmed by the following summary of a Return of Houses in England and Wales assessed to House Duty in 1861–2 ; with the addition of the rest of the 1,110,000 houses occupied by the Middle Classes, given in page 14.

Classification by houses.
Mr. Locke King, Commons Return, 428, 1863.

HOUSES AND RENTAL OF THE UPPER AND MIDDLE CLASSES,
ENGLAND AND WALES.

	Number.
I. *Large Houses—*	
(1) £200 and upwards Rent	9,800
(2) £100 to £200	32,800
II. *Middle Houses –*	
£50 to £100	102,000
III. *Small House—*	
(1) £20 to £50	375,400
(2) £10 to £20	590,000
Total Houses .	1,110,000

CHAP. III. This table requires a moment's consideration to point out its results and bearing. The number of persons with incomes of their own, including lodgers, ladies, and younger persons still living with their families, is nearly twice the number of houses, or two persons with incomes for each house. But two persons of £5,000 and upwards a year seldom, or never, live in the same house. On the contrary, each has one house at least, and very commonly two or even more, in different parts of the country, though at different rents. Hence the number of large houses is likely to exceed the number of large incomes, so that the proportion of 9,800 large houses to 7,500 large incomes is like the truth, and each confirms the correctness of the other.

In the next class of incomes the same causes tend to increase the numbers near the top of the scale ; but other causes come into play, diminishing the number near the £1,000 limit. Persons with that income in the country frequently live in smaller houses, and lodgers begin to appear. The proportion of 32,800 houses from £100 to £200 rent, appears to tally with the 42,000 incomes from £1,000 to £5,000 a year, and with the smaller houses occupied by the highest class.

In the incomes below £1,000, the number of lodgers, ladies, and inmates of family houses increases rapidly, so that the proportions of the houses below £100, viz. 102,000, 375,000 and 590,000, appear to confirm the number of incomes below £1,000, viz. 150,000, 850,000 and 1,000,000.

It is, of course impossible to suggest anything Importance of beyond a general and approximate correspondence. corroboration. No amount of income, in different parts of the country, and in classes of persons of different habits, corresponds strictly with any amount of house-rent. But where strict proof is impossible, and in a matter of such social interest and even political importance, approximate indications are of great value, and ought not to be neglected. And their trustworthiness is very much increased when independent indications corroborate each other.

CHAPTER IV.

CHAP. IV. WE now approach a question of great difficulty, and which has been the subject of keen controversy—

Sources of information. the wages or earnings of the Manual Labour Class. Much information has been collected from time to time in the Miscellaneous Statistics of the Board of Trade, and in papers read by Mr. Purdy, Mr. Chadwick, and others, and especially in the elaborate estimates published last year by Professor Leone Levi. I have made use of all these authorities, after testing them by my own inquiries. As regards the rate of wages, I have found Professor Levi's book very accurate and fair. The averages which I have adopted are rather lower than his, but this may be owing to the fall of wages since the period of his investigation. Like him, I have in most instances included the value of board and lodging, although in some cases the propriety of doing so is doubtful. For example, why should a seaman be credited with three shillings or four

shillings a week for lodging—exclusive of food ? Chap. IV.
He cannot navigate the ship without sleeping in it,
and the vessel does not cost a penny the more for
giving him berth-room. So also with female house
servants; their sleeping in the house is, in most
cases, a necessity, without which the house, like the
ship, could not be worked.

Another point is the age at which a manual Age of su-
labourer ceases to be an effective. I am afraid that tion.
perannua-
60 years is about the average ; six or seven years
earlier than the Middle Classes. After that age
a man becomes unfit for hard work ; and if he
loses his old master, cannot find a new one. In
some trades, a man is disabled at 55 or 50. A
coal-backer is considered past work at 40. I have Mayhew,
London
endeavoured to be on the safe side by taking 65 as Labour,
vol. iii. p.
the termination of their working life, and have 253.
excluded all above that age from my calculation
of wages.

But the most important point of all is the allow- Deduction
for loss of
ance which must be made for what workmen call work.
"playing ;" that is to say, being "out of work,"
from whatever cause, whether forced or voluntary.
It is here that I am at issue with Professor Levi. Levi,
Wages,
He estimates the lost time at no higher average than &c. p. 5.
4 weeks out of the 52, and thinks it sufficiently
covered by omitting from the wage-computation all

Chap. IV. workmen above 60 years old, *i.e.* the non-effectives. If this were the real state of things, England would be a perfect Paradise for working men! If every man, woman, and child returned as a worker in the census had full employment, at full wages, for 48 weeks out of the 52, there would be no poverty at all. We should be in the Millennium! Far other is the real state of affairs; and a very different tale would be told by scores and even hundreds of thousands, congregated in our large cities, and seeking in vain for sufficient work.

Building trades.

I will take a good average instance (and a very large one) of the way in which wages are earned in the building trades. These trades form a whole, and include carpenters, bricklayers, masons, plasterers, painters, and plumbers, and number, in England and Wales, about 387,000 men above 20 years of age. In London their full time wages average 36s. a week. In the country they are lower, 30s. to 28s. or 26s.; growing less the farther we go northward. The full-work average may be taken at 30s. But it is only the best men, working for the best masters, that are always sure of full time. These trades work on the hour system, introduced at the instance of the men themselves, but a system of great precariousness of employment. The large masters give regular wages to their good workmen, but the smaller masters, CHAP. IV. especially at the East end of London, engage a large proportion of their hands only for the job, and then at once pay them off. All masters, when work grows slack, immediately discharge the inferior hands, and the unsteady men, of whom there are but too many even among clever workmen, and do not take them on again till work revives. In bad times there are always a large number out of employment. In prosperity much time is lost by keeping Saint Monday, and by occasional strikes. There are also 40,000 men between 55 and 65 years of age, who, in the building trade, are considered as past hard work, and who suffer severely by want of employment. There are also the sick and the paupers, all of whom are included in the muster-roll of the census. The effect of all these causes is to produce an immense margin of lost time, and a great reduction from the nominal or full time wages.

Let us turn to another great branch of industry, Agricul-tural Labourers. the Agricultural Labourers: whose numbers are, men, 650,000 ; boys, 190,000 ; women, 126,000 ; and girls, 36,000. Continuous employment has largely increased since the New Poor Law of 1834, and good farmers now employ their men regularly. But in many places such is not the custom. Near

CHAP. IV. Broadstairs, in Kent, I was told that, on an average, labourers are only employed 40 weeks in the year.

Mr. Purdy, Statistical Journal, vol. xxiv. p. 353. Mr. Purdy's figures of the influence of the seasons on agricultural employment, show that the wages paid in the second quarter of the year, on a large estate in Notts, were 20 per cent. more than in the first quarter. In the harvest quarter, they were more than double. He also mentions the significant fact, that the pauperism of the five most agrarian divisions of England is greater in February than in August, by 425,000 against 370,000, or 55,000 persons. These 55,000 represent a great prevalence of the custom of turning off labourers at the slack season. So that, even so far as the men are concerned, there must evidently be a large deduction for time out of work. But when we come to boys and women, the case is still stronger. I found in Kent and other places, that boys and women's employment is very irregular; and that they are not at work more than half their time. In fact, they are employed as supernumeraries to the p. 372. men, and only taken on at busy times. Mr. Purdy gives in his paper a table of the earnings of a labourer's family, at Bolton Percy, near York, in 1842. The man had constant work, but the wife was only employed 210 days in the year, and the boy 223 : being about two-thirds of their time.

Deductions like these make a heavy per centage, CHAP. IV. when they occur more or less over an area of 234,000 boys and women.

We will now take the iron trade, and the large Iron trade, class of miners, comprising together nearly 450,000 and miners. men and boys. They all have a particular propensity for strikes, and sometimes their masters vary the programme by a lock-out. The Middlesbro' iron-workers struck last year for 18 weeks, or more than one-third of the year. The South Yorkshire and Derbyshire Miners almost always have a strike on hand in some part of the district. This is in prosperous times. In bad times there is much slackness of work.

Turn next to the cotton manufacture, including Cotton 143,000 men, 82,000 boys, 150,000 women, and manufac- ture. 121,000 girls; altogether, 496,000. We all know their periodical distresses. It may be said that these were accidents. They are not mere accidents, but incidents, natural incidents, of our manufacturing economy. They are sure to recur under different forms; either from gluts, or strikes, or war; and they must be allowed for in computations of earnings.

I come lastly to instances from trades at the East Lon- East end of London, where I have lately had a don. great deal of experience. It is there that the

CHAP. IV. struggle for existence is most intense, from London being the resort and refuge of the surplus population of other parts of the country. The London Dock labourers earn, when on full time, 15s. a week; but so great is the competition that even in ordinary years they are employed little more than half their time. During the past year 5s. a week has been considered tolerably lucky.

Dock
labourers.

Silk-weavers are in chronic distress. The men's nominal wages are 12s. a week; but their real earnings do not average more than 6s.

Silk-
weavers.

Cabinet-makers stand well in the list of trades, their nominal wages for the kingdom being set down at 30s. a week. But the cabinet-makers at the East end, a very numerous body, are in what is called the "slop trade," and are ground down by the dealers, who own what are called "slaughter-houses," in which they take advantage of the necessities of the small manufacturers (expressively called "garret masters") and compel them to sell their upholstery at little above the cost of materials. Between dealers and want of work, I am told that numbers of the "slop" cabinet-makers are not earning 7s. 6d. a week.

Cabinet-
makers.

None but those who have examined the facts can have any idea of the precariousness of employment in our large cities, and the large pro-

portion of time out of work, and also, I am bound CHAP. IV.
to add, the loss of time in many well-paid trades
from drinking habits. Taking all these facts into
account, I come to the conclusion, that for loss of
work from every cause, and for the non-effectives
up to 65 years of age, who are included in the Rule of
deduction
census, *we ought to deduct fully* 20 *per cent.* 20 per
cent.
from the nominal full-time wages.

I will cite one more fact in confirmation. The Average
pauperism.
average number of paupers at one time in receipt England
and Wales.
of relief in 1866 was 916,000, being less than for
any of the four preceding years. The total number
relieved during 1866 may, on the authority of a
Return of 1857, given in the Appendix, be calculated at $3\frac{1}{2}$ times that number, or 3,000,000.
All these may be considered as belonging to the
16,000,000 of the Manual Labour Classes, being
as nearly as possible 20 per cent. on their number.
But the actual cases of relief give a very imperfect idea of the loss of work and wages. A large
proportion of the poor submit to great hardships,
and are many weeks, and even months, out of
work before they will apply to the Guardians.
They exhaust their savings, they try to the utmost
their trade unions or benefit societies ; they pawn
little by little all their furniture ; and at last are
driven to ask for relief. I am not astonished at

CHAP. IV. their reluctance, for what do they get? After waiting in a crowd and in the most humiliating publicity, they get an order for the stoneyard, with 6*d.* a day, and a loaf per week of bread for each of their family. Sometimes, rather than accept the relief, they die of starvation.

Masters, Foremen, and Overlookers. One more point requires a brief mention. The census does not distinguish masters and overlookers, or foremen, from their workmen. The masters must be taken from the table of 1851, which gave 129,000 as the number in that year. I have deducted their numbers in each case from the totals in 1861. The overlookers and foremen are nowhere estimated, but in many of the returns of workmen and wages given in the Miscellaneous Statistics for 1866, they will be found to be 3 and 4 per cent. I am told that in the building trade they are more numerous than the masters. I have estimated their numbers at 100,000. There can be no doubt that they are not Manual Labourers, and that they were rightly classed by the Government in the Electoral Returns of 1866 as belonging to the Middle Classes.

Miscellaneous Statistics, 1866, part vi. p. 278, &c.

Estimate of wages, Appendix IV. I now come to the present numbers of the Manual Labour Class, and their wages. A detailed estimate will be found in Appendix IV. In order to throw them into a connected form, I have grouped the different employments by the wages earned by the men above 20 years of age. This gives an intelligible principle, and brings together the similar employments in a manner easy to remember.

It is a curious fact, that in the great majority of occupations the average wages of a boy, a woman, and a girl, added together, amount to those of a man. For instance, in the first class, where the men's average wages are 35*s.* a week, the boys' are 10*s.*, the women's 8*s.* 6*d.*, and the girls' 6*s.* 6*d.*, total 35*s.* But this does not hold good in some light occupations, where skill of fingers is required; or in the case of house servants.

In calculating the earnings I have given the full-work average wages, and deducted 20 per cent. from the total of 52 weeks for out of work, sick, and paupers; except in Sub-division vi., where I have deducted 10 per cent. only from the wages of the male agricultural labourers, and 33 per cent. from those of the boys and women; and except also in the case of house servants, where I have deducted only 10 per cent., and of soldiers, where I have deducted nothing.

The following table gives a summary of the Manual Labour Class and their earnings in the briefest possible form. The weekly wages men-

E

CHAP. IV. tioned are the average full-work scale ; but the annual earnings are the net average receipt after all deductions for loss of work, sick, and paupers.

The Manual Labourers appear to group naturally into three great classes, with minor subdivisions.

MANUAL LABOUR CLASSES.

ENGLAND AND WALES.

CLASS IV.

HIGHER SKILLED LABOUR AND MANUFACTURES.

Men's Weekly Wages 28s. to 35s. and Net Annual Earnings £60 to £73.

1. Instrument Makers and Engine Drivers, 35s.

2. Books; Iron and other Manufactures; Building Trades; Ships; Bread, 28s. to 30s.

Men, 840,800 ; *Boys,* 219,400 ; *Women,* 40,300 ; *Girls,* 22,500— TOTAL, 1,123,000.

CLASS V.

LOWER SKILLED LABOUR AND MANUFACTURES.

Men's Weekly Wages 21s. to 25s., and Net Annual Earnings £46 to £52.

3. Carriers by Water; Coaches and Harness; Hardware and other Manufactures, 25s.

4. Carriers by Land ; Servants ; Cotton ; Woollen and other Manufactures ; Shoemakers ; Tailors, and other Trades ; Miners, 21s. to 23s.

Men, 1,610,000 ; *Boys,* 494,000 ; *Women,* 1,083,000 ; *Girls,* 632,000—TOTAL, 3,819,000.

CLASS VI.

AGRICULTURE AND UNSKILLED LABOUR.

Men's Weekly Wages, 12s. to 20s. and Net Annual Earnings £20 to £41.

5. Public Service ; Rural Manufactures and Gloves ; Quarries ; Animals ; Docks and Porters, 15s. to 20s.
6. Agriculture ; other Labourers, 14s.
7. Soldiers ; and Silk Manufacture, 12s.
8. Laundresses and Needlewomen, 12s.

Men, 1,516,800 ; *Boys,* 476,700 ; *Women,* 666,500 ; *Girls,* 183,000—TOTAL, 2,843,000.

The Number and Earnings are worked out in Tables 1 and 2 of Appendix IV., in eight subdivisions, and the result is shown in the following general summary :—

SUMMARY OF NUMBER AND EARNINGS, 1867.

ENGLAND AND WALES.

CLASS.	Persons.	Net Annual Earnings, less all Deductions.
IV.—Higher Skilled Labour and Manufactures	1,123,000	£ 56,149,000
V.—Lower Skilled Labour and Manufactures	3,819,000	127,921,000
VI.—Agriculture and Unskilled Labour	2,843,000	70,659,000
TOTAL	7,785,000	£254,729,000

This table shows at a glance how much the Middle Class of lower skilled labour and manu-

CHAP. IV. factures exceeds both in numbers and earnings
either of the other two classes.

It also shows how far the two Upper Classes, or
skilled labour and manufactures, exceed the com-
bined forces of unskilled labour and agriculture.
In numbers, the two first classes are nearly
5,000,000 against the third class with less than
3,000,000, or 1⅔ to 1. In earnings they are
£184,000,000 against £71,000,000, or 2½ to 1.

The total Income and Income Classes of England
and Wales will thus be :—

ENGLAND AND WALES, 1867.

GROSS INCOME OF ALL CLASSES.

	Persons with Independent Incomes.	Amount of Incomes.
		£
Upper and Middle Classes	2,053,000	407,200,000
Manual Labour Class	7,785,000	254,729,000
TOTAL	9,838,000	£661,929,000

This Income gives an average to the persons of
independent income of £68.

But it is usual to calculate taxation and income
per head of population. By this standard, the total
income of England and Wales will give an average
of nearly £32 to each of the 21,000,000 of her
present population.

CHAPTER V.

INCOME OF SCOTLAND.

THE separate existence of the three divisions of CHAP. V. the United Kingdom, England, Scotland, and Ireland, increases very seriously the toil of our investigation, and may render it more tedious to the reader. Less than half the labour would have been required for a consolidated country like France. But it has the advantage of enabling us to study, separately, portions of the country which differ in their inhabitants and mode of life, and of compelling a more thorough acquaintance with our native land.

Scotland had, in 1861, a population of 3,062,000 ; Comparison with or rather more than one-seventh of the population England. of England. But she is a poorer country, and paid Income Tax in 1865 on only £30,816,000 ; or one-tenth of the income of £309,175,000 which during the same year was charged in England. For the ten preceding years, her income increased at the same proportional rate as that of England ;

CHAP. V. having been charged, in 1855, upon £22,000,000 when England paid upon £225,000,000. Like England also, her progress was most rapid from 1863 to 1865, her increase during those three years having been £3,000,000 corresponding to a contemporaneous increase of £33,000,000 in England. The estimate of income of the Upper and Middle Classes in 1867 will be as follows :—

Upper and Middle Class Incomes.

UPPER AND MIDDLE CLASS INCOMES, 1867.

	£
1. Income Tax was charged in 1865 on	30,816,000
2. The increase for the two years since 1865 may be taken at	1,500,000
So that the total amount charged in 1867 would be	32,316,000

This amount, at the average in Schedule D of £278, would be paid by 116,000 persons. But there are 272,000 persons of the Upper and Middle Classes with independent incomes, allowing 8,000 for the 3 per cent. increase since 1861 ; so that 156,000 are not included in the Income Tax.

3. Unreturned profits under Schedule D estimated at 10 per cent. on £11,000,000	1,100,000
4. The aggregate amount of £60 a year excused to persons with less than £100 a year	1,300,000
5. The 156,000 Incomes under £100 a year who do not pay Income Tax, at £50 each	7,800,000
Making the total Income of the Upper and Middle Classes	42,516,000

Manual Labour Class Incomes.

The earnings of the Manual Labour Class have been calculated by occupations and classes in the

same manner as for England. Their numbers in Chap. V.
1867, with 3 per cent. increase, are 1,122,000.
The rate of wages has been taken for men and
women at an average of 2s. per week less than in
England, and for boys and girls 1s. to 1s. 6d. less ;
with exceptions in the case of agricultural labourers
and the linen manufacture. The deductions are
the same as for England. Their total earnings are
thus estimated at £31,746,000

Dividing the Income subject to Income Tax in Total Scotch Incomes.
the same proportion as Schedule D, and the
earnings of the Manual Labour Class into the
same three groups of occupations as in England,
the total Scotch Income appears as follows :—

Gross Income of Scotland, 1867.

UPPER AND MIDDLE CLASSES.	Assessments and Persons.	Amount.
CLASS I.—*Large Incomes.*		£
(1) £5,000 a year and upwards	600	10,068,000
(2) £1,000 to £5,000 . . .	4,100	8,505,000
II.—*Middle Incomes.*		
£300 to £1,000	13,900	7,464,000
III.—*Small Incomes.*		
(1) £100 to £300	97,400	8,679,000
(2) Under £100	156,000	7,800,000
TOTAL . . .	272,000	£42,516,000
MANUAL LABOUR CLASS.		
IV.—*Higher skilled Labour and Manufactures.*		
Men's average, £56 to £68 10s.	137,000	6,454,000
V.—*Lower skilled Labour and Manufactures.*		
Men's average, £41 10s. to £48.	558,000	16,543,000
VI.—*Agriculture and unskilled Labour.*		
Men's average, £16 10s. to £32	427,000	8,750,000
TOTAL . . .	1,122,000	£31,747,000
GRAND TOTAL	1,394,000	£74,263,000

Average Incomes per head.   This gives an average Income of £53 for every person with an independent Income or earnings; and an average per head on the total population of 3,150,000, of £23 10s.

CHAPTER VI.

INCOME OF IRELAND.

IRELAND presents a singular phenomenon—a de-
creasing population and an increasing income. The
population diminished from 8,196,000 in 1841 to
6,574,000 in 1851, or at the rate of nearly 20 per
cent. ; and again diminished in 1861 to 5,799,000,
being nearly at the rate of 12 per cent. Dr. Farr
has kindly furnished me with the official estimate
of the population in the middle of 1867, at
5,557,000, or a further diminution of 4 per cent.
The Income Tax was only imposed in 1853, but the
value of the property charged rose from £21,086,000
in 1855 to £24,438,000 in 1865 ; or an increase of
16 per cent. Wages have also considerably risen.

Yet Ireland is the poorest of the three kingdoms.
Her population is one-fourth of the estimated
21,000,000 of England, but her income chargeable
to Income Tax is only one-twelfth of that of
England. Her population is nearly double that of
Scotland, and yet her income chargeable to Income

CHAP. VI. Tax is £6,000,000 less than that of Scotland. But it will be seen that her total income is greater than that of Scotland. The income of her Upper and Middle Classes is as follows :—

UPPER AND MIDDLE CLASS INCOMES, 1867.

	£
1. Income Tax was charged in 1865 on . .	24,438,000
2. The increase since 1865 may be taken at .	300,000
So that the total amount charged in 1867 would be	24,738,000
This amount, at the average in Schedule D of £258, would be paid by 96,000 persons, leaving 338,000 of the Upper and Middle Classes with independent incomes who do not pay Income Tax (allowing for 4 per cent. decrease).	
3. Unreturned profits under Schedule D estimated at 10 per cent. on £5,300,000 . .	500,000
4. The aggregate amount of £60 a year excused to persons with less than £100 a year . .	1,000,000
5. The 338,000 Incomes under £100 a year, who do not pay Income Tax, at £40 each .	13,520,000
Total Income of the Upper and Middle Classes	£39,758,000

The earnings of the Manual Labour Class have been calculated by Occupations and Classes in the same manner as for England and Scotland. Their numbers in 1867, allowing for 4 per cent. decrease, are 2,054,000. The rates of wages has been taken for men at an average of 5s. per week less than in England, except in the cotton industry, where they,

as well as women, boys, and girls, are taken at the
same rate as in England; and at an average of 3s.
less for women, except domestic servants, taken at
5s. less, and in agriculture, where they are taken at
1s. 6d. less than in England ; and at an average of 1s.
less for boys and 1s. 6d. for girls, except in domestic
service, where the girls are taken at 3s. 6d. less.
The deductions are the same as for England. Their
total earnings are thus estimated at £38,169,000.

Dividing the Income subject to Income Tax in
the same proportion as Schedule D (an average
of £258), and the earnings of the Manual Labour
Class into the same three groups of occupations
as in England and Scotland, the total income of
Ireland is :—

GROSS INCOME OF IRELAND, 1867.

UPPER AND MIDDLE CLASSES.	Assessments and Persons.	Amount.
CLASS I.—*Large Incomes.*		£
(1) £5,000 a year and upwards	400	4,985,000
(2) £1,000 to £5,000	2,700	5,379,000
II.—*Middle Incomes.*		
£300 to £1,000.	14,400	7,347,000
III.—*Small Incomes.*		
(1) £100 to £300	78,500	8,527,000
(2) Under £100	338,000	13,520,000
TOTAL	434,000	39,758,000
MANUAL LABOUR CLASS.		
IV.—*Higher skilled Labour and Manufactures.*		
Men's average, £50 to £62 10s.	85,000	3,750,000
V.—*Lower skilled Labour and Manufactures.*		
Men's average, £35 to £41 10s.	710,000	16,188,000
VI.—*Agriculture and unskilled Labour.*		
Men's average, £10 10s. to £26	1,259,000	18,231,000
TOTAL	2,054,000	38,169,000
GRAND TOTAL	2,488,828	£77,927,803

This division of the population and income shows
a great divergence of type from England and Scotland. Both these countries have a large accumulation of wealth in the highest class of incomes; and
in the Manual Labour Class a great preponderance in
the centre class of the most important manufactures

and lower skilled labour. But in Ireland the highest Chap. vi. fortunes are smallest in aggregate amount, and each descending Upper and Middle Class of Income increases in its total. Similarly in the Manual Labour Classes, highly skilled labour is very small in amount; and the agricultural and unskilled labour class is the largest, both in numbers and income.

The average income for each person of independent means is £31, and for each person of the whole estimated population of 5,567,000 is £14. The table of average income for the three kingdoms may be interesting.

AVERAGE INCOMES OF ENGLAND, SCOTLAND, AND IRELAND.

	Average for each person of independent income or Wages.	Average per head of the Population.
	£	£
England	68	32
Scotland	53	$23\frac{1}{2}$
Ireland.	31	14

CHAPTER VII.

INCOME OF THE UNITED KINGDOM.

Cʜᴀᴘ.ᴠɪɪ. WE are now able to add together the aggregate Incomes of England, Scotland, and Ireland, and to obtain the Income of the United Kingdom. The totals of the Upper and Middle Classes and Manual Labour Class are (in thousands)—

UNITED KINGDOM, 1867.

Gross
Income.

GROSS INCOME.

	Persons with In-dependent Income, or Wages.	Amount.
		£
Upper and Middle Classes . .	2,759,000	489,474,000
Manual Labour Class	10,961,000	324,645,000
	13,720,000	814,119,000

In round numbers their earnings are £490,000,000 and £325,000,000, and the total £814,000,000 ; an amount exceeding all previous calculations of the Income of the nation. It is a wonderful thing that the

gross annual income of the United Kingdom should CHAP.VII.
exceed by £36,000,000 the whole £778,000,000 of
the National Debt. I say gross income, because
there is a fallacy in taking the amount which
we have obtained, as Net Income, counted once
over.

The totals for the Upper and Middle Classes and Its magni-
for the Manual Labour Class are not less surprising. tude.
Without inquiring closely into the details, it is
almost impossible to believe the aggregate results.
I must own that this was my own case in 1866,
when Mr. Gladstone stated that the aggregate income
of the working classes exceeded £250,000,000. I
am glad to have the opportunity of confirming his
calculation. There may be many now incredulous
as to the income of the Upper and Middle Classes,
but I have no fear of the continuance of their un-
belief. Estimating the income of a great and
wealthy nation without careful study is like at-
tempting to guess the number of grains of sand on
the sea-shore, or the drops of water in a river;
conjecture falls far short of the actual reality.

It is necessary to repeat for the United Kingdom Table of
the table which has been used for England, Scotland, Gross
Income.
and Ireland.

UPPER AND MIDDLE CLASSES—	Assessments and Persons.	Amount.
Class I.—*Large Incomes.*		£
(1) £5,000 and upwards . .	8,500	126,157,000
(2) £1,000 to £5,000 . . .	48,800	83,324,000
II.—*Middle Incomes.*		
£300 to £1,000	178,300	87,723,000
III.—*Small Incomes.*		
(1) £100 to £300 . . .	1,026,400	110,950,000
Below Income Tax.		
(2) Under £100 . . .	1,497,000	81,320,000
Total . . .	2,759,000	£489,474,000
MANUAL LABOUR CLASS—		
Men's average Wages.		
IV.—*Higher Skilled Labour and Manufactures.*		
£50 to £73	1,345,000	66,353,000
V.—*Lower Skilled Labour and Manufactures.*		
£35 to £52	5,087,000	160,652,000
VI.—*Agriculture and Unskilled Labour.*		
£10 10s. to £36	4,529,000	97,640,000
Total . . .	10,961,000	£324,645,000
Grand Total	13,720,000	£814,119,000

The £5,000 Incomes include £30,000,000 Incomes of 400 Companies respecting which see page 36.

It is worth observing that the £100 line divides CHAP. VI
the total Income into two nearly equal portions of
£408,000,000 and £406,000,000. It may be called
the equatorial line of British income.

Figures give so imperfect an idea of actual pro- Diagram
portions that I have endeavoured to realize them in title-page.
opposite
the accompanying diagram; which represents accu-
rately by spaces of *half an inch square* each *third
of* £1,000,000 belonging to any class of Income;
and distinguishes the Upper and Middle from the
Manual Labour Incomes. The waving line of de-
marcation between the two classes shows that part
of the latter class rise in their amount of incomes
above some of the Upper and Middle Classes.

It may be useful to ascertain how far this National Income
Income is derived from Capital, and how far from from Capital and
Profits and Earnings. The income of the capital Profits and
Earnings.
possessed by the Manual Labour Class is so small
that for this purpose it may be disregarded. The
capital possessed by the Upper and Middle Classes
may be estimated from the Income Tax. Schedules
A and C are wholly Capital, and Schedule D con-
tains a considerable amount of income from Capital
in foreign property and undertakings, and in English
companies. Trades and professions require working
capital, the interest on which, in the opinion of Appendix
V.
competent judges, amounts to one-fifth of their gross Table 3.

F

CHAP. VII. income. By these simple rules I arrive at an estimate, the details of which are worked out in the Appendix, showing the proportions as follows :—

ESTIMATED INCOME FROM CAPITAL AND FROM PROFITS AND EARNINGS.

UNITED KINGDOM, 1867.

	£
From Capital—	
Upper and Middle Classes	280,000,000

From Profits and Earnings—	£	
Upper and Middle Classes . . .	209,500,000	
Manual Labour Class	324,500,000	
		534,000'000
TOTAL .		£814,000,000

So that about *one-third* of the total income is derived from Capital; *two-thirds* from Profits and Earnings.

Previous estimates. NOTE.—The previous estimates of Income of the United Kingdom have been :—

	£
1801	230,000,000
1822—Lord Liverpool . .	{ 250,000,000 to 280,000,000 }
1841	450,000,000
1848—Mr. Ray Smee (adding 52 millions for Ireland)	540,000,000
1858—Professor Leone Levi . . .	600,000,000

And in 1866 Professor Levi estimated the Income of the *Working Classes* at £418,000,000.

CHAPTER VIII.

SOURCES AND NET AMOUNT OF THE INCOME OF THE UNITED KINGDOM.

WE have still to inquire what are the great depart- Chap. VIII.
ments of industry from which this income is derived,
and to ascertain which of them are independent
sources of wealth, and which only apparent sources
with a second-hand income derived from the con-
tributions of the rest.

Occupations have been classed by political econo- Productive
and Non-
mists in two categories : the Productive, such as productive
Classes.
agriculture or manufactures,—and the Non-productive, such as the army or domestic service. But
many occupations partake of both these characters,
and cannot without violence be classed entirely with
either one or the other. The occupation of Conveyance by Land or Water is one of this kind. A very
large portion of its functions are non-productive, in
conveying persons or things for pleasure, or for
mere change from one place to another. In another

portion conveyance acts simply as a retailer, by carrying goods from the depôt when they are complete and at their standard price, to the customer or sub-customer. In the third portion alone is it quasi-productive, by enabling articles to reach the general market. Another instance is the class of tradesmen or dealers. To a certain extent they produce, but to a very great extent they simply retail, and for so doing reimburse themselves by a tax beyond the standard value of their wares, and so impose a burden on the community. Production appears to me to cease at the moment when it has lodged the product in the hands of the wholesale dealer. The product has then contributed its maximum addition to the wealth of the nation, and is so much currency, capable of realizing a certain value, whether sent abroad or retained for home consumption. But, after that point, every additional agent or retailer diminishes its power of supplying the national wants. The retail dealer is in the nature of a servant, who is paid to fetch and distribute the articles of which there is need.

Auxiliary Class.   For these reasons I suggest an intermediate class for occupations of a mixed character, and which, from the aid it often lends to production, I should call the *Auxiliary Class*. I should also place in this class the income derived from houses, which are for the most part connected but indirectly with production.

The classification into Productive and Non-pro- ductive is in reality of a superficial character, and inaccurate, because every class contributes some- thing towards production. The soldier who guards industry, and the maid-servant who sets free her master for productive labour, as truly aid in pro- duction as the labourer himself. The physician who heals, the lawyer who arranges disputes, the clergyman whose secular office is to promote virtue and morality, each fulfil an important function, without which the machinery of work would be impeded or stopped. Even the butterflies of fashion, so completely the creatures of idleness, re- present the most important of all the elements of production—the element of capital. It would be more accurate to classify the different occupations into the two heads of Productive and Auxiliary, and to drop the term Non-productive.

But for the purpose of distinguishing the income that is an original and fresh contribution to the common stock from that which is merely derived from the first, the three terms afford a useful dis- tinction. By income of the Productive Classes I mean income that is the earnings of production, the money received in exchange for the material products of the nation's toil; and which is generally a new acquisition to the nation's property. By income of the Non-productive Classes I mean income paid out of the first income for services not directly productive, and which appears twice over in the total income of the two classes. By income of the Auxiliary Classes I mean income which in some instances belongs to the first of of these classes, and in others to the second; and which sometimes receives first-hand, and sometimes second-hand or derived income. Take as an example, £10,000 worth of carpets made in Halifax for the French market. The price obtained at the French port is divided between the manufacturer and his workmen, the railway and steamboat, and the agents engaged in transmission. The net amount, say £6,000 after deduction of materials, forms part of their income, and appears in its proper place in the income assessed to Income Tax or in manual wages. In this instance the railway is productive. But the manufacturer and his workmen pay out of this income, wages to servants, fees to doctors and lawyers, and fares to railways for pleasure trips (the railway in this case being non-productive); and the income so paid out appears a second time in the account of income and earnings. So also with respect to houses; the rent of the manufactory is first-hand income paid as rent to the owner out of the original £10,000, before passing through any previous income ; the rent of the manufacturer's house and the operatives' cottages is second-hand, and comes out of their income.

This is simple enough, but the difficulty arises in considering the subsequent circulation of the money. Do not the operatives and their master pay out of their income for corn and manufactured goods ; and will not the income of the farmer and the cloth or cotton manufacturer be also second-hand, like the doctor's ? The answer appears to be that the wealth of a nation must be chiefly spent in feeding and clothing its individual members. The carpet manufacturers in reality exchange a part of their original carpet income for an original corn income, and another part for an original cloth income ; and yet all three sorts of income are rightly set down as first-hand or fresh wealth of the nation. But the services of the doctor give no original product in exchange, and are simply paid by a deduction out of the carpet income. The nation produces, say, £500,000,000 worth of calico, cloth, machinery, corn, and other goods, the twelve months' yield of her industry, which is for the most part credited to the producers as income, and out of which all her population have to live. They

CHAP. exchange amongst each other, eat part, are clothed
VIII.
with part, sell to other nations, and get cash for
part, and store up savings and capital. But the
Auxiliary and Non-productive Classes have for the
most part to be fed out of this income fund, and
so far their income is credited over again in the
national balance-sheet. I want to separate the
two, and to show what is the original income-fund
of the nation.

The classes of income to be distinguished are :—

I. *Of the Productive Classes*, derived from agriculture, mining,
manufactures, or wholesale trade, and colonial and foreign property and
loans.—For the Upper and Middle Classes it is found in Schedules A
and B, part of Schedule C, and in Schedule D, excluding the retail
trade. Among the Manual Labour Class, it includes the great bulk of
their earnings, excluding only those named under the other two heads.

II. *Of the Auxiliary Classes*, derived from houses, conveyance,
and the retail trade.—For the Upper and Middle Classes it is for the
most part assessed under houses, railways, and canals in Schedule A,
and under trading profits in Schedule D. It also includes a very large
number of clerks, shopmen, and women, with income under £100
a year. From the Manual Labour Class it includes the building trade
and persons engaged on railways, roads or water, and employed by
dealers in food.

III.—*Of the Non-Productive Classes*, from the public service, professions, and domestic employments ; and also from fundholders in
the Stocks of Great Britain, whose income is a mere debt from the
nation.—It is comprised in Schedule E, and in part of Schedules
C and D ; and includes the earnings of soldiers, sailors, police,
and servants.

From these data it is possible to form an approximate division of the Income of the United

Kingdom between these three classes. It is worked CHAP.
VIII. out in the Appendix, and gives the following result :—

PRODUCTIVE, AUXILIARY, AND NON-PRODUCTIVE CLASSES.

UNITED KINGDOM, 1867.

		Amount of Income.
I. *Productive Classes.*	£	£
Agricultural	165,764,000	
Manufacturing, Mining, &c.	313,866,000	
		479,630,000
II. *Auxiliary Classes*		196,000,000
III. *Non-Productive Classes*		138,370,000
		£814,000,000

Thus the gross annual income of the country is £814,000,000, or £36,000,000 more than the whole National Debt.

The productive income from agriculture and manufactures, the fund in which all the National Income is first received, is £480,000,000, and may be considered as original earnings.

The Auxiliary Classes have an income of £196,000,000, partly original earnings, and partly second-hand, paid out of original earnings.

The Non-Productive Classes have an income of £138,000,000, entirely second-hand, and paid out of original earnings.

The Net Income of the United Kingdom, the original earnings out of which the nation provides

CHAP.
VIII. food and clothing, and pays all taxes and expenses, may be taken at from £550,000,000 to £600,000,000 a year. The second-hand or dependent income, which is paid out of the original earnings, and gives a deceptive magnitude to the national income roll, is from £260,000,000 to £210,000,000. And besides this, part of the net income consists of local industries, which depend for their existence on the prosperity of the larger manufactures. If any disaster happens to the principal means of production—as a food famine in an agricultural country, or a cotton famine in a manufacturing district, or a money famine in a city of miscellaneous industry—the ruin of the chief producers brings with it the collapse of the Auxiliary Classes and local trades. Retail dealers lose their business, railways their traffic, house-proprietors their rent, and all the minor employments are stopped. Every failure of the income of the Productive Classes causes an additional loss of more than half the amount in the rest of the community. The blow has a multiplying power. The Income of England is the largest of any nation, and shows wonderful good fortune and prosperity; but we must not forget that it rests on an unstable foundation. The turn of trade, or obstinacy and short-sightedness in our Working Classes, or a great naval

war, may drive us from the markets of the world, Chap. VIII. and bring down our Auxiliary as well as our Productive industries. In our present complex civilization, the effect of such a calamity on a large scale can hardly be imagined. We might see our national income disappear far more rapidly than it has increased, and a period of suffering among our population of which no cotton famine or East London distress can afford an adequate idea. The Roman generals in their triumphal processions had a monitor upon their car to remind them of their mortality; and a similar moral ought not to be forgotten in relating the triumphs of British industry.

England's position is not that of a great landed proprietor, with an assured revenue, and only subject to occasional loss of crops or hostile depredations. It is that of a great merchant, who by immense skill and capital has gained the front rank, and developed an enormous commerce, but has to support an ever-increasing host of dependents. He has to encounter the risks of trade, and to face jealous rivals, and can only depend on continued good judgment and fortune, and the help of God, to maintain himself and his successors in the foremost place among the nations of the world.

APPENDIX I.

APPENDIX II.

APPENDIX III.

APPENDIX IV.

APPENDIX V.

APPENDIX I.

TABLE 1.

CLASSIFICATION OF POPULATION, ENGLAND AND WALES, 1861.

PERSONS WITH INDEPENDENT INCOMES.	Under 20 years of age.	Above 20 years.	Total.	Per contage of Total.
I. *Upper and Middle Classes*—(Table 5.)				
Males	136,301	1,194,232	1,330,533	
Females	30,047	582,534	612,581	
Total	166,348	1,776,766	1,943,114	10
II. *Manual Labour Classes*—(Table 6.)		Above 20 years and under 65.		
Males	1,151,141	3,655,232	4,806,373	
Females.	823,608	1,715,746	2,539,354	
Total	1,974,749	5,370,978	7,345,727	37
Total persons of Independent Incomes . .	2,141,097	7,147,744	9,288,841	47
PERSONS WITHOUT INDEPENDENT INCOMES. III.—(Table 7.)		Above 20 years.		
Males	3,254,456	333,455	3,587,911	
Females.	3,671,164	3,367,418	7,038,582	
Total	6,925,620	3,700,873	10,626,493	53
GRAND TOTAL accounted for .	9,066,717	10,848,617	19,915,334	100

Appendix I.

TABLE 2.
SCOTLAND.—CENSUS, 1861.

PERSONS WITH INDEPENDENT INCOMFS.	Under 20 years of age.	Above 20 years.	Total.	Per centage of Total.
I. Upper and Middle Classes —				
Males	20,950	168,089	189,039	
Females	3,024	71,953	74,977	
Total	23,974	240,042	264,016	8.6
		Above 20, and under 65 years.		
II. Manual Labour Class—				
Males	161,845	514,993	676,838	
Females . . .	128,376	284,081	412,457	
	290,221	799,074	1,089,295	35.6
Total	314,195	1,039,116	1,353,311	44.2
PERSONS WITHOUT INDEPENDENT INCOMES.		Above 20 years.		
III.				
Males	529,079	54,892	583,971	
Females	567,316	557,696	1,125,012	
Total	1,096,395	612,588	1,708,983	55·8
Grand Total .	1,410,590	1,651,704	3,062,294	100·0

TABLE 3.
IRELAND.—CENSUS, 1861.

PERSONS WITH INDEPENDENT INCOMES.	Under 20 years of age.	Above 20 years.	Total.	Per centage of Total.
I. Upper and Middle Classes—				
Males	23,954	274,378	298,332	
Females	6,999	147,431	154,430	
Total	30,953	421,809	452,762	7·8
		Above 20 years, and under 65.		
II. Manual Labour Class—				
Males	320,654	1,115,630	1,436,284	
Females	233,128	506,365	739,493	
Total	553,782	1,621,995	2,175,777	37.5
Total persons with Indepentent Incomes . .	584,735	2,043,804	2,628,539	45·3
PERSONS WITHOUT INDEPENDENT INCOMES.		Above 20 years.		
III.				
Males	951,900	150,854	1,102,754	
Females	1,037,457	1,030,249	2,067,706	
Total	1,989,357	1,181,103	3,170,460	54·7
Grand Total .	2,574,092	3,224,907	5,798,999	100·0

TABLE 4.

METHOD OF CLASSIFICATION OF POPULATION.

Upper and Middle Classes.	Manual Labour Classes.	Dependent Classes (without income).
General Rules.	*General Rules.*	*General Rules.*
ALL Persons of Rank and Property. Officers. Agents. Learned Professions. Mercantile Men. Dealers, tradesmen, and persons who buy or sell. Owners. Masters and Mistresses. Superintendents. Collectors. Foremen. Measurers. Clerks. Shopmen.	ALL Workmen and Labourers. Servants. Soldiers. Seamen. Pensioners. Drivers. Warehousemen. Artificers. (Except Foremen and Superintendents).	ALL Wives (not otherwise described). Children and Relatives at home. Scholars. Paupers. Prisoners. Vagrants. Manual Labour Classes above sixty-five years old.
Special Cases.	*Special Cases.*	*Special Cases.*
Sub-order.	*Sub-order.*	*Sub-order.*
1. One-third Police. 4. One-half Widows (not otherwise described). 8. Two-thirds Farmers and Graziers, and their Sons, &c. Their Wives, 19,000. One-half Farm Bailiffs.	1. Two-thirds Police. 8. Farmers and Graziers and their Sons, Wives, Daughters, &c. one-third. One-half Farm Bailiffs.	4. One-half Widows (not otherwise described). 8. Farmers and Graziers' Wives, 90,000. Their Daughters, &c. two-thirds.
11. Masters, 32,000; Mistresses, 30,000. 12. One-half Males and all Females in Animal Food, less Butchers' Wives. One-half Males and and all Females in Vegetable Food. Three-fourths Males and all Females in Drinks and Stimulants.	11. One-half Shoemakers' Wives. 12. One-half Males in Animal and Vegetable Food. One-fourth Males in Drinks and Stimulants.	11. One-half Shoemakers' Wives. 12. Butchers' Wives.

G

TABLE 5.

ENGLAND AND WALES, 1861.

UPPER AND MIDDLE CLASSES,
WITH INDEPENDENT INCOMES.

Census Class and Order.	MALES		FEMALES.	
	Under 20.	20 and upwards.	Under 20.	20 and upwards.
I. Professional—				
1. Government . .	1,889	50,497	194	3,720
2. Army and Navy Officers . . .	1,341	13,340	—	—.
3. Learned Professions	23,150	146,815	16,678	76,020
II. Domestics—				
4. Widows. . . .	—	—	34	134,537
5. Board and Lodging	709	72,627	949	84,849
III. Commercial—				
6. Persons who buy or sell	23,414	130,820	1,864	27,545
7. Conveyance . .	3,825	23,590	69	2,190
IV. Agricultural—				
8. Land.	3,143	218,431	297	49,780
9. Animals . . .	1,201	16,377	3	121
V. Industrial—				
10. Art and Mechanic productions . .	3,620	76,471	293	26,854
11. Textile and Dress	12,800	71,100	—	30,000
12. Food and Drinks.	31,306	176,308	5,351	51,958
13. Animal substances	—	400	—	—
14. Vegetable substances . . .	1,714	14,161	575	2,108
15. Minerals . . .	5,108	56,297	1,459	3,184
VI. Indefinite—				
16. Miscellaneous . .	2,750	4,459	1,493	3,027
17. Rank or Property	331	22,539	788	86,641
Foremen, Overlookers, and Timekeepers	—	100,000	—	—
	136,301	1,194,932	30,047	582,534

TABLE 6.

ENGLAND AND WALES, 1861.

MANUAL LABOUR CLASS,
EARNING INDEPENDENT WAGES.

Census Class and Order.	MALES.		FEMALES.	
	Under 20.	20 to 65.	Under 20.	20 to 65.
I. Professional—				
1. Government . .	1,894	28,036	—	—
2. Soldiers & Sailors	17,864	91,842	—	—
II. Domestic—				
5. Servants . .	38,765	94,672	383,022	649,643
III. Commercial—				
7. Conveyance . .	89,377	300,367	2,603	3,726
IV. Agricultural—				
8. Land	309,483	879,391	40,759	127,285
9. Animals . . .	10,863	53,576	73	144
V. Industrial—				
10. Art and Mechanic Productions . .	151,522	621,097	10,569	20,975
11. Textile and Dress	200,671	559,315	350,953	869,162
12. Food and Drinks .	24,000	107,180	—	—
13. Animal Substances	8,538	37,684	2,539	4,000
14. Vegetable Sub-stances . . .	19,248	83,162	5,969	9,295
15. Minerals . . .	223,158	643,801	23,617	26,927
VI. Indefinite—				
16. Labourers, &c. .	55,758	255,109	3,504	4,589
	1,151,141	3,655,232	823,608	1,715,746

TABLE 7.

ENGLAND AND WALES, 1861.

PERSONS WITHOUT INDEPENDENT INCOMES OR WAGES.

Class and Order.	MALES.		FEMALES.	
	Under 20.	20 and upwards.	Under 20.	20 and upwards.
II. Wives, Children, Scholars, and Widows . . .	3,250,845	12,288	3,648,341	3,012,893
IV. Farmers' Wives and all Daughters, &c.	—	—	19,129	126,758
V. Half Shoemakers' Wives . . .	—	—	—	40,000
Butchers' Wives .	—	—	153	25,144
VI. Tramps	—	2,000	—	—
Prisoners, Vagrants, Criminals, &c. .	3,611	16,971	3,541	53,870
Manual Labour Classes above 65 years of age .	—	302,196	—	108,753
	3,254,456	333,455	3,671,164	3,367,418

NOTE. The Tables for Scotland and Ireland have been worked out in the same way.

APPENDIX II.

NUMBER AND AVERAGE INCOME OF INCOME-TAX PAYERS,

ENGLAND AND WALES.

In calculating the number of Income Tax payers, it is necessary to remember that those who appear as paying on less than £100 a year, have other income for which they appear in other Schedules ; and that only one of these appearances ought to be taken into account.

The information respecting the numbers charged is not given in all the Annual Reports, and the proportions must be taken from different years.

Schedule B is given for 1858-9 in the Commons Return, 300, 1860. The income charged to duty was £26,600,000 ; and the persons charged on incomes above £100 was 54,000 ; below £100, 207,000.

Schedule C was found to be paid in 1850 on £27,000,000 by 204,000 persons. But examination of 21,000 accounts in Consols showed that only one-fourth were above £100 a year. Assuming this proportion for the rest,

Schedule E in 1864 was charged on £17,487,000, paid by 97,600 persons, of whom 67,000 had more than £100 a year.

Schedule D in 1864 was charged on £95,600,000, and paid by 297,000 persons, of whom 246,000 had above £100 a year.

Schedule A is paid in the first instance by the occupiers, and no means exist of ascertaining the actual number of owners who ultimately bear it. The income charged in 1864 was £125,000,000, and this on the same scale of individual income as Schedule D would be paid by 379,000 persons, of whom 314,000 would have £100 a year.

The total income for these Schedules and years was £292,000,000 ; and the payers with more than £100 a year were 731,000.

The number of payers under a £100 a year was 504,000 ; of whom one-third at least appear also among the first 731,000, and half the remainder, or one-third of the whole (169,000), will be the net number to be added.

Hence the total number of tax-payers for the £292,000,000 will be 900,000 ; giving an income of £323 each ; being nearly the same as the average for Schedule D.

But, in consequence of the number of English Companies, I have taken the average for England and Wales at only £306.

In the net number so obtained there will be, besides those just mentioned, a large number of persons who appear twice or oftener : such as merchants and professional men assessed under Schedule D, who also pay more than £100 under Schedule A as landed proprietors or owners of houses ; or under Schedule B on a farm ; or under Schedule C as fundholders in British or Colonial Stocks. It is roughly estimated that these duplicate and triplicate appearances balance the number who are omitted through their assessments being made upon their partnership.

APPENDIX III.

TOTAL ANNUAL PAUPERS.

By the kindness of Mr. Purdy, of the Statistical Department of the Poor Law Board, I have been furnished with the only return in existence of total annual Paupers.

It was for the parochial year 1857 :—

Paupers, indoor and outdoor, relieved during the half-year ending Michaelmas, 1856 . . .	1,845,782
„ „ „ *only* on 1st July, 1856	796,102
Paupers, indoor and outdoor, relieved during the half-year ending Lady-day, 1857 . . .	1,934,286
„ „ „ *only* on 1st Jan., 1857	843,430
The apparent total for the two half-years is .	3,780,068
But from this must be deducted the whole number of Paupers relieved on Michaelmas-day, 1856—say	800,000
Leaving the net total	2,980,000
Being 3½ times the number on the 1st January.	

Mr. Purdy, in the discussion before the Statistical Society, maintained that a greater deduction ought to be made than the whole number of paupers on Michaelmas-day. But I am unable to see how this can be.

APPENDIX IV.

MANUAL LABOUR CLASSES,
ENGLAND AND WALES, 1867.

TABLE I.

CLASSIFICATION AND ESTIMATED NUMBERS.

CLASS IV.

HIGHER SKILLED LABOUR AND MANUFACTURES.

SUBDIVISION I. Men's Weekly Wages, 35s.	Numbers.	Net Annual Earnings, less Deductions for Loss of Work, Sick, & Paupers.
MEN—		£
(a) Makers of complicated instruments, such as Opticians, 1,500 ; Philosophical Instrument Makers, 1,000 ; Scale Makers, 1,150 ; Surgical Instrument Makers, 650 ; Leather Case Makers, 2,200 ; Watch Makers, 15,400 ; Gold, Silver, and Precious Stones, 11,000	32,900	
(b) Engine Drivers	9,300	
	42,200	
BOYS, 10,500 ; WOMEN, 2,300 ; GIRLS, 1,800	14,600	
TOTAL	56,800	3,366,800

Instrument makers and Engine drivers.

CLASS IV.—*continued.*

SUBDIVISION II. Men's Weekly Wages, 28s. to 30s.	Numbers.	Net Annual Earnings, less Deductions for Loss of Work, Sick, & Paupers.	
MEN—		£	
(a) Printers, 19,200 ; Bookbinders and Bookfolders, 5,000 ; Lithographers, &c. 4,150	28,350		Books.
(b) Manufacturers of Hats, 9,000 ; Comb, Bone, and Ivory, 3,000 ; Wood Carving and Toys, 6,500 ; other Workers in Wood, 4,100 ; Earthenware, 20,300 ; Glass, 9,700 ; Iron, 91,700 ; Cutlery (Arms and Tools), 44,250 ; Musical Instruments, 2,200 ; Cabinet Makers and Upholsterers, 39,000	229,750		Iron and other manufactures.
(c) Carpenters, 136,000 ; Builders, 9,900 ; Brickmakers, 29,000 ; Bricklayers, 65,000 ; Masons, 69,600 ; Slaters, 4,500 ; Plasterers, 14,500 ; Paper Hangers, 1,900 ; Painters, 57,200 . . .	387,600		Building trades.
(d) Shipbuilders and Shipwrights, 35,000 ; Sawyers, 28,000 ; Coopers, 14,500 ; Turners, 5,400	82,900		Ships.
(e) Bakers' Workmen, 30,000 ; Butchers' Men, 40,000	70,000		Bread and meat.
	798,600		
BOYS, 208,900 ; WOMEN, 38,000 ; GIRLS, 20,700	267,600		
TOTAL SUBDIVISION . . .	1,066,200	52,782,200	
TOTAL OF CLASS IV.	1,123,000	£56,149,000	

CLASS V.

LOWER SKILLED LABOUR AND MANUFACTURES.

	SUBDIVISION III. Men's Weekly Wages, 25*s.*	Numbers.	Net Annual Earnings, less Deductions for Loss of Work, Sick, & Paupers.
	MEN—		£
Carriers by water.	(*a*) Carriers on Canals, Bargemen, and Watermen, 29,300 ; Warehousemen, 15,200 ; Seamen, 100,000	144,500	
Coaches and harness.	(*b*) Hair Dressers, 8,000 ; Coach Makers, 16,000 ; Harness Makers, 14,000	38,000	
Hardware and other manufactures.	(*c*) Manufacturers of Machines and Implements, 80,000 ; Hosiery, 20,000 ; Lace, 6,700 ; Mixed Materials, 8,000 ; Tobacco, 2,900 ; Linen, 7,100 ; Patterns and Umbrellas, 5,500 ; Paper, 12,000 ; Ropes, 7,300 ; and other articles in Hemp, 4,000 ; Soapboilers, 1,260 ; Tallow Chandlers, 3,000 ; Skinners, 1,400 ; Tanners, 7,200 ; Curriers, 10,600 ; Oilmen, Polishers and Japanners, 8,500 ; Workers in Bark, Cane, Rush and Straw, 11,000 ; Salt, 1,700 ; Whitesmiths, Blacksmiths, and Hardware, 130,000 ; Copper, 4,400 ; Tin and Quicksilver, 13,000 ; Zinc and Lead, 3,500 ; Brass and Mixed Metals, 30,000 ; Gas Works, 8,000 ; Dockyard Work, 12,470	399,500	
		582,000	
	BOYS, 143,500 ; WOMEN, 93,000 ; GIRLS, 57,700	294,200	
	TOTAL SUBDIVISION . . .	876,200	32,182,500

Class V.—*continued.*

SUBDIVISION IV. Men's Weekly Wages, 21s. to 23s.	Numbers.	Net Annual Earnings, less Deductions for Loss of Work, Sick, & Paupers.	
Men—		£	
(a) Carriers on Roads, 56,700 ; Coachmen and Cabmen, 25,000 ; Letter Carriers, 11,500 ; Railway Servants and Police, 25,500 ; Railway Labourers, Platelayers, Navvies, 39,000	157,700		Carriers by land.
(b) Servants, 98,600 ; Coalheavers, 11,600 ; Chimney Sweepers, 4,300 ; Waterworks, 1,800	116,300		Servants.
(c) Cotton, Calico and Fustian, 143,000 ; Wool and Worsted, 95,000 ; Sugar Refiners, 2,600 ; Chemical, 15,000	255,600		Cotton, Woollen, and other manufactures.
(d) Boot and Shoe (workmen), 157,000 ; Millers, 20,000 ; Brush Makers, 7,000 ; Tailors, 83,000	267,000		Shoemakers, Tailors, &c.
(e) Miners—Coal, 173,000 ; Copper, 12,000 ; Tin, 9,000 ; Lead, 14,000 ; Iron, 20,000 ; other Mines, 5,500 . . .	233,500		Miners.
	1,030,000		
Boys, 350,500 ; Women, 296,000 ; Girls, 187,500	834,000		
Maidservants, 692,000 ; Do. Girls, 386,800	1,078,800		
Total Subdivision. . .	2,942,800	92,738,500	
Total of Class V.	3,819,000	£127,921,000	

Class VI.

UNSKILLED LABOUR AND AGRICULTURE.

	SUBDIVISION V. Men's Weekly Wages, 16s. to 20s.	Numbers.	Net Annual Earnings, less Deductions for Loss of Work, Sick, & Paupers.
	Men—		£
Public service.	(a) Seamen, R.N. 12,540 ; Mariners, 7,000 ; Militia, 2,400 ; Coast Guard, 3,800 ; Police, 14,500 ; Government Messengers and Workmen, 2,100 . . .	42,340	
Rural manufactures.	(b) Straw, 1,820 ; Gloves, 2,700 ; Maltsters and Brewers, 25,000	29,520	
Quarries.	(c) Stone, 18,000 ; Slate, 7,000 ; Limestone, 4,700	29,700	
Animals.	(d) Horsekeepers, Gamekeepers, and Drovers, 44,000 ; Fishermen, 50,000 . .	94,000	
Docks and Porters.	(e) Dock Labourers, 29,500 ; Messengers and Porters, 35,300	64,800	
		260,360	
	Boys, 89,700 ; Women, 45,000 ; Girls, 24,280	158,980	
	Total Subdivision . . .	419,340	11,922,800
	SUBDIVISION VI. Men's Weekly Wages, 14s.		
	Men—		
Agriculture.	(a) Agricultural Labourers, Shepherds, and Farm Servants, 880,040	880,040	
Labourers.	(b) Labourers, 258,000 ; Road Labourers and Scavengers, 10,500 . . .	268,500	
		1,148,540	
	Boys, 364,700 ; Women, 127,000 ; Girls, 36,110	527,810	
	Total Subdivision . . .	1,676,310	£42,313,400

Appendix IV. 93

CLASS VI.—*continued.*

SUBDIVISION VII. Men's Weekly Wages, 12s.	Numbers.	Net Annual Earnings, less Deductions for Loss of Work, Sick, & Paupers.	
MEN—		£	
(a) Soldiers, 56,000 ; Chelsea and Greenwich Pensioners, 17,400	73,400		Soldiers.
(b) Silk Manufacture, 34,500 . . .	34,500		Silk manufacture.
	107,900		
BOYS, 22,300 ; WOMEN, 47,300 ; GIRLS, 25,140	94,740		
TOTAL SUBDIVISION . . .	202,640	4,220,800	
SUBDIVISION VIII. Women's Weekly Wages, 12s.			
WOMEN— Laundresses, 149,008 ; Milliners and Dressmakers, 213,504 ; Shirtmakers and Seamstresses, 63,094 ; Staymakers, 9,571 ; Bonnet Makers, 5,094 ; Cap Makers, 3,013 ; Furriers, 1,043 ; Button Makers, 2,000 ; Fancy Workers, 1,043 .	447,200		
GIRLS	97,470		
TOTAL SUBDIVISION . . .	544,670	£12,202,000	
TOTAL OF CLASS IV.	2,843,000	£70,659,000	

N.B. The way in which these earnings are calculated is shown in the following Table.

Appendix IV.

TABLE 2.

EARNINGS BY CLASSES.—England and Wales.

Class IV.

HIGHER SKILLED LABOUR AND MANUFACTURES.

Subdivision.	Number.	Full work Average Weekly Wages.	Average Annual Income, less out of work, Sick, and Paupers.	Total Amount.	Total of Classes.
			s.		£
I. Men . . .	42,200	35s. 0d.	73 0	3,080,600	
Boys . . .	10,480	10s. 0d.	21 0	220,080	
Women . .	2,290	8s. 6d.	18 0	41,220	
Girls . . .	1,800	6s. 6d.	13 10	24,300	
Total . .	56,770				3,366,200
II. Men . . .	798,600	28s. to 30s.	60 0	47,916,000	
Boys . . .	208,900	9s. 0d.	18 10	3,864,650	
Women . .	38,000	9s. 6d.	19 0	722,000	
Girls . . .	20,700	6s. 6d.	13 10	279,450	
Total . .	1,066,200				52,782,300

Class V.

LOWER SKILLED LABOUR AND MANUFACTURES.

Subdivision.	Number.	Full work Average Weekly Wages.	Average Annual Income, less out of work, Sick, and Paupers.	Total Amount.	Total of Classes.
			£ *s.*	£	£
III. Men . . .	582,000	25s. 0d.	52 0	30,264,000	
Boys . . .	143,740	8s. 0d.	16 10	2,371,710	
Women . .	93,000	9s. 6d.	19 0	1,767,000	
Girls . . .	57,780	6s. 6d.	13 10	780,030	
Total . .	876,520				35,182,740
IV. Men . . .	1,028,000	23s. to 21s.	46 0	47,288,000	
Boys . . .	350,530	7s. 6d.	15 10	5 433,210	
Women . .	296,000	10s. 0d.	21 0	6,216,000	
Girls . . .	187,560	6s. 0d.	12 10	2,344,500	
Maid Servants	694,160	14s. 0d.	32 10	22,560,200	
Do. Girls . .	386,810	11s. 0d.	23 0	8,896,630	
Total . .	2,943,060				92,738,540
				Carried forward . .	£184,069,780

Class VI.

UNSKILLED LABOUR AND AGRICULTURE.

Subdivision.	Number.	Full work Average Weekly Wages.	Average Annual Income, less out of work, Sick, and Paupers.	Total Amount.	Total of Classes.
					£
			Brought forward .		184,069,780
			£ s.	£	
V. Men . . .	260,360	20s. to 15s.	36 10	9,503,140	
Boys . .	89,700	6s. 6d.	13 10	1,210,950	
Women .	45,200	9s. 0d.	18 10	830,500	
Girls . .	24,280	7s. 6d.	15 10	376,340	
					11,922,930
Total . .	419,340				
VI. Men . . .	1,148,500	14s. 0d.	33 0	37,900,500	
Boys . .	364,700	4s. 6d.	8 0	2,917,600	
Women .	127,000	5s. 6d.	9 10	1,206,500	
Girls . .	36,110	4s. 6d.	8 0	288,880	
					42,313,480
Total . .	1,676,310				
VII. Men . . .	{ 73,400 34,500	14s. 6d. 10s. 0d.	30 0 } 20 0	2,892,000	
Boys . .	22,280	6s. 0d.	12 10	278,500	
Women .	47,300	7s. 0d.	14 10	685,850	
Girls . .	25,140	7s. 0d.	14 10	364,530	
					4,220,880
Total . .	202,620				
VIII. Women .	447,200	12s. 0d.	25 0	11,180,000	
Girls . .	97,340	5s. 0d.	10 10	1,022,070	
					12,202,070
Total . .	544,540				
			GRAND TOTAL . .		£254,729,140

APPENDIX V.

TABLE 1.

INCOME OF UPPER AND MIDDLE CLASSES, 1867,
ARRANGED BY SCHEDULES OF INCOME TAX.

UNITED KINGDOM.

	Income charged 1865.	Estimated Increase.	Unreturned Income Tax.	Total, 1867
	£	£	£	£
Schedule A . .	154,119,000	8,500,000	—	162,619,000
Schedule B . .	35,564,000	500,000	—	36,064,000
Schedule C . .	330,71,000	1,000,000	—	34,071,000
Schedule D . .	120,148,000	4,000,000	17,600,000	141,748,000
Schedule E . .	21,528,000	—	—	21,528,000
	£364,430,000	£14,000,000	£17,600,000	£396,030,000
Incomes excused as under £60			1867. 12,300,000	
Incomes under £100			81,320,000	
				93,620,000
			TOTAL. . .	£489,650,000

The above Table is used in Tables 3 and 4.

Appendix V.   97

TABLE 2.

INCREASE OF CAPITAL—1855 TO 1865.

The increase of *Income from Capital charged to Income Tax* from
1855 to 1865 was—

		£
Schedule A (all the increase)		37,650,000
„	B (one-fifth of the increase—see p. 65)	1,050,000
„	C (all the increase)	7,300,000
„	D (all increase of foreign property and one-fifth remainder) . . .	16,000,000
		£62,000,000

Capitalized at an average of 5 per cent., this gives 1,240 *millions
sterling* as the increase of Capital actually charged to Income Tax in
1865 over that in 1855.

TABLE 3.

ESTIMATE OF INCOME DERIVED FROM CAPITAL
AND FROM PROFITS AND EARNINGS.

	£	£
Capital—		
Schedule A, Lands, Houses, Mines,' &c. (all)	162,500,000	
Schedule B, Farming Profits, one-fifth (being interest on the capital employed by the farmer)	7,200,000	
Schedule C, Public Funds (all)	34,000,000	
Schedule D,		
(1) Foreign Property and Undertakings, and Capital in some English Companies (estimate)	30,000,000	
(2) One-fifth of Profits in remainder of Schedule	22,800,000	
Incomes excused as below £60 and Incomes below £100	23,500,000	
(One-fourth may be taken, including incomes from land or personal property as well as the proportion of profits by the preceding rule)		280,000,000
Profits and Earnings—		
Schedule B, remainder, or four-fifths	28,800,000	
Schedule D, remainder	89,000,000	
Schedule E, Public Offices and Annuities	21,500,000	
Incomes excused, and Incomes below £100 remainder	70,200,000	
Manual Labour Class (all)	324,500,000	
		534,000,000
TOTAL		£814,000,000

TABLE 4.

PRODUCTIVE, AUXILIARY, AND NON-PRODUCTIVE INCOMES.

UNITED KINGDOM, 1867.

I. PRODUCTIVE CLASSES.

(1.) AGRICULTURE.

Schedule A. Lands . . .	55,500,000	
„ *B.* (all) . . .	36,064,000	
Incomes excused as under £60 } See Table 1. *Incomes under £100 . . .* }		
The number of persons is about 22½ per cent. of the Upper and Middle Classes with Incomes.		
Taking this proportion of the Total Income of £93,600,000	21,000,000	
Agricultural Labourers (Wages in Summary)	53,200,000	
		165,764,000

(2.) MANUFACTURES, MINING, MONEY, &c.		
Schedule A. Miscellaneous	16,118,000	
„ *C.* Colonial and Foreign Funds (estimate)	14,000,000	
„ *D.* All except Professions and Retail Trade .	107,748,000	
Incomes excused as under £60 } See Table 1. *Incomes under £100 . . .* }		
The number of persons is about 22½ per cent. of the Upper and Middle Classes with Incomes.		
Taking this proportion of Total Income of £93,600,000	21,000,000	
Manual Labour Class employed in Manufactures and Mining (Wages in Summary)	155,000,000	
		313,866,000
Carried over .		£479,630,000

Brought forward .   £479,630,000

II.—AUXILIARY CLASS.

Schedule A. — Houses, Railways, and
    Canals £91,000,000
  "   B.—Retail Trades (estimate) 14,000,000

Incomes excused as under £60 } See Table 1.
Incomes under £100 . . }

 The number of persons is about 31 per
cent. of the Upper and Middle Classes
with Incomes.
 Taking this proportion of Total Income
of £93,600,000 29,000,000

Manual Labour Class.
 Building Trade, Conveyance, and Food
 (Wages in Summary) . . 62,000,000
           ——— 196,000,000

III.—NON-PRODUCTIVE CLASSES.

Schedule C (British Funds) . . 20,071,000
 "   *D* (professional men) . . 20,000,000
 "   *E* (all) 21,528,000

Incomes excused as under £60 } See Table 1.
Incomes under £100 . . . }

 The number of persons is about 24 per
cent. of the Upper and Middle Classes
with Incomes.
 Taking this proportion of Total Income
of £93,600,000 . . . 22,620,000
Manual Labourers—
 Public Service and Domestic (Wages in
 Summary) 54,151,000
          ——— 138,370,000
          £814,000,000

www.ingramcontent.com/pod-product-compliance
Lightning Source LLC
Chambersburg PA
CBHW030550270326
41927CB00008B/1592

9 7 8 3 3 3 7 1 3 7 5 8 8